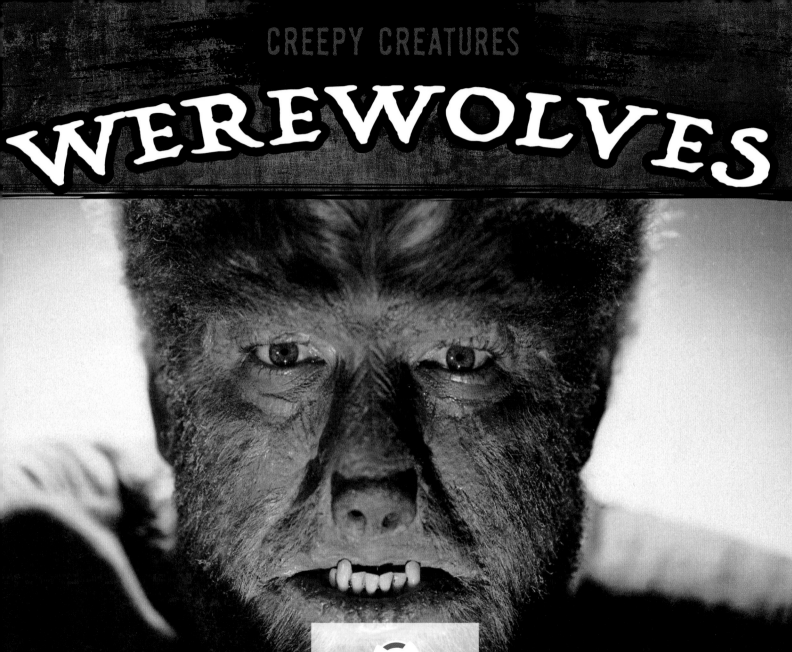

CREEPY CREATURES

# WEREWOLVES

Sarah Tieck

Big Buddy Books
An Imprint of Abdo Publishing
abdopublishing.com

**abdopublishing.com**

Published by Abdo Publishing, a division of ABDO, PO Box 398166, Minneapolis, Minnesota 55439.
Copyright © 2016 by Abdo Consulting Group, Inc. International copyrights reserved in all countries. No part
of this book may be reproduced in any form without written permission from the publisher. Big Buddy Books™
is a trademark and logo of Abdo Publishing.

Printed in the United States of America, North Mankato, Minnesota.
042015
092015

Cover Photo: John Kobal Foundation/Getty Images.
Interior Photos: © AF archive/Alamy (pp. 24, 25); Ann Ronan Pictures/Glow Images (p. 11); Archive Photos/Getty
    Images (p. 22); Associated Press (p. 23); Buyenlarge/Getty Images (p. 21); DEA/W. BUSS/Getty Images
    (p. 27); Deposit Photos (p. 9); © HAMMER HAMMER FILM PRODUCTIONS/Ronald Grant Archive/Alamy (p. 22);
    ©iStockphoto.com (pp. 5, 7, 15, 19, 29, 30); Michael Ochs Archives/Getty Images (p. 17); Movie Poster Image
    Art/Getty Images (p. 24); © North Wind Picture Archives (p. 11); © Photos 12/Alamy (p. 9); Shutterstock.com
    (p. 13).

Coordinating Series Editor: Rochelle Baltzer
Contributing Editors: Tamara L. Britton, Bridget O'Brien, Marcia Zappa
Graphic Design: Jenny Christensen

**Library of Congress Cataloging-in-Publication Data**

Tieck, Sarah, 1976- author.
  Werewolves / Sarah Tieck.
      pages cm. --  (Creepy creatures)
   ISBN 978-1-62403-768-9
1.  Werewolves--Juvenile literature.  I. Title.
   GR830.W4T54 2016
   398.21--dc23
                          2015004204

# Contents

# Creepy Werewolves

People love to tell spooky stories, especially about creepy creatures such as werewolves. The stories describe their hairy bodies and thirst for blood. They say werewolves howl under a full moon!

Werewolves have appeared in books, stories, plays, television shows, and movies. But are they real, or the stuff of **legend**? Let's find out more about werewolves, and you can decide for yourself!

Wolves and werewolves are known for their strong eyesight. It helps them find and catch prey.

5

# Scary Stories

According to **legend**, werewolves are humans who can change into wolves. This can happen when the moon is full or when the sun goes down. Werewolves grow sharp teeth. Their bodies become covered with hair. Some werewolves can see in the dark. Like wolves, they can growl or howl.

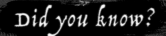

### Did you know?

There are ways to tell if people are werewolves. They might have sharp teeth and pointy nails. And some say, a wound would reveal hair under their skin.

Some believe the full moon has special qualities that affect wolves and werewolves.

People become werewolves in different ways. Some are bitten or scratched by a werewolf. Others are turned by magic or are born into a werewolf family.

Sometimes, a werewolf can be turned back into a regular human. People may speak the werewolf's name or hit it on the head. Other times, a werewolf cannot be turned back into a human. To stop the werewolf, people may have to kill it.

Like wolves, werewolves have sharp teeth to catch and eat their prey.

The most common way to kill a werewolf is with an object made of silver. This may be a bullet, blade, or knife.

# Around the World

Stories of people changing into animals are found in many **cultures**. The idea of the man-wolf is most common in European countries, including Germany and France.

People started to fear those they believed to be werewolves. Being a werewolf was a crime. Those accused of it were arrested or killed.

### Did you know?

The French word for "wolf" is *loup*. Old French stories call werewolves *loup-garou* (loo-guh-ROO).

Wolves and werewolves have appeared in art from France (*left*) and Germany (*below*).

The animal form that a person becomes varies by location. In Africa, people may change into lions or hyenas. In India and other parts of Asia, people become tigers or foxes.

Native Americans, particularly Navajo, tell stories of skinwalkers in North America. These witches could become any animal by wearing its dead skin. They had glowing red eyes and left large footprints. People feared skinwalkers.

African were-hyenas are different from real hyenas (*above*). They are often called *bouda* and feed on humans. In human form, they may have reddish eyes and very hairy bodies.

# Living History

No one knows exactly why or how werewolf **legends** started. But, stories of werewolves go back thousands of years. In a Greek myth, the god Zeus changes King Lycaon into a wolf. Later, wolves with human **qualities** appeared in fairy tales, such as *Little Red Riding Hood*.

## Did you know?

The Greek word for "wolf" is *lykos*. Werewolves are also called *lycanthropes*.

The story of *Little Red Riding Hood* is about a girl and a big bad wolf who wants to eat her.

Werewolf movies became popular over the years. One of the first was the 1935 horror film *Werewolf of London*. Another scary movie called *The Wolf Man* came out in 1941. Later, werewolves appeared in funny and scary television shows and movies.

Lon Chaney Jr. starred as the Wolf Man. The Wolf Man loved the character played by Evelyn Ankers.

# Good or Evil?

In many stories, werewolves are monsters to be feared. Many have **superhuman** strength or speed. They are not the same in wolf form as they are in human form. As werewolves, they are hungry for flesh and blood.

When werewolves get angry they become stronger.

Some stories are about good werewolves. Since they have human intelligence and **superhuman** strength, they can help others.

Whether a werewolf is good or evil, it may still harm others. So, people work to stop them. If a werewolf is wounded as a wolf, it will be wounded as a human. This makes the werewolf easier to find. Then, a person may do a **spell** to stop the werewolf from changing into wolf form.

In 1985's *Teen Wolf*, Michael J. Fox played a good werewolf. As a human, he was nerdy Scott Howard. As a werewolf, he used his superhuman strength to help his basketball team win.

# The Werewolf of Paris

*The Werewolf of Paris* is a book by Guy Endore. It was printed in 1933 and tells the life story of a werewolf. Movies such as 1961's *The Curse of the Werewolf* were based on this book.

# Werewolves in Pop Culture

## Remus Lupin

Werewolf characters, such as Remus Lupin, are part of J.K. Rowling's Harry Potter books. In these stories, werewolves change when the moon is full. David Thewlis played Remus Lupin in the movies.

## Scooby-Doo! and the Reluctant Werewolf

Shaggy becomes a werewolf in this 1988 television movie. He races Dracula and other famous monsters. And Scooby and his friends help him become human again.

## Werewolf of London

In this 1935 movie, Dr. Wilfred Glendon becomes a werewolf after being attacked on a trip to Tibet. The only cure is an unusual flower.

# Jacob Black

In the Twilight Saga by Stephenie Meyer, Jacob comes from a family of werewolves. He uses his wolf **instincts** and strength to help save Bella's life. In the movies, Taylor Lautner played Jacob.

## Did you know?

In 2011, MTV began a series called *Teen Wolf*. It is based on the 1985 movie.

# Fact or Fiction?

   People have feared werewolves for hundreds of years. Today, most people do not believe werewolves are real.

   But, there is a mental illness called lycanthropy (leye-KAN-thruh-pee). People who have lycanthropy believe they really are werewolves or some other animal. Special doctors can help them to stop thinking this way.

## Did you know?

A doctor first reported lycanthropy in 1852 in France. The patient was a man who thought he was a wolf. He only wanted to eat raw, rotten meat.

In the 1500s, there was an especially widespread fear of werewolves in France. Thousands of people believed to be werewolves were locked in jails like this one to keep others safe.

Entrée par la Cour

# What Do You Think?

So, what do you think about werewolves? Do they still send a chill up your spine? It can be fun to watch spooky movies about werewolves or to dress as werewolves on Halloween.

It is also interesting to learn about werewolves. Knowing what is true and what is made up is powerful. Read some **fiction** about werewolves, or discover their history. You are in for an interesting journey!

During a full moon, werewolves come out. If one scratches a human, he or she may become a werewolf too.

# Let's Talk

What examples of werewolf stories can you think of?

What would you do if you had to fight a werewolf?

How do you think it would feel to be a werewolf? How would you protect the people you cared about during a full moon?

If you were to write a story about a werewolf, how would you explain your character becoming a werewolf?

Imagine that someone you love became a werewolf. Is there any way this could be a good thing?

# Glossary

**culture** (KUHL-chuhr) the arts, beliefs, and ways of life of a group of people.

**fiction** stories that are not real.

**instinct** a way of behaving, thinking, or feeling that is not learned, but natural.

**legend** an old story that many believe, but cannot be proven true.

**quality** a feature that someone or something has.

**spell** words with magic powers.

**superhuman** above or beyond human power, size, or ability.

# Websites

To learn more about Creepy Creatures, visit **booklinks.abdopublishing.com**. These links are routinely monitored and updated to provide the most current information available.

# Index